Your
INTELLIGENT
HEART

Kathy—
Best wishes for
continuing the spirit of
your Intelligent Heart!
Susan B. Wilson

Your
INTELLIGENT
HEART

Notes to
Women
Who Work

Susan B. Wilson

amacom

American Management Association

New York • Atlanta • Boston • Chicago • Kansas City • San Francisco • Washington, D.C.
Brussels • Mexico City • Tokyo • Toronto

This book is available at a special
discount when ordered in bulk quantities.
For information, contact Special Sales Department,
AMACOM, a division of American Management Association,
135 West 50th Street, New York, NY 10020.

Library of Congress Cataloging-in-Publication Data
Wilson, Susan B.
    Your intelligent heart : notes to women who work / Susan B.
Wilson.
        p.   cm.
    Includes bibliographical references (p.   ).
    ISBN 0-8144-0274-7
    1. Women—Psychology.   2. Women in business—Psychology.
3. Women in business—Life skills guides.   I. Title.
HQ1206.W727   1995
646.7' 0082—dc20
                                                        95-23773
                                                            CIP

Printing number

10   9   8   7   6   5   4   3   2

"*Your Intelligent Heart* will inspire and motivate all readers to discover and share the very best of themselves."

—Jack Canfield, author of *Chicken Soup for the Soul* and
A Second Helping of Chicken Soup for the Soul

"*Your Intelligent Heart* provides timeless strategies that transcend many of the trendy management philosophies seen in the popular press. The author engages the reader in a thoughtful dialogue."

—Suzanne Liberty, Ph.D., Dean of the Graduate School
and Director of Research, Clarkson University

"This book is a 'feel good' reading experience. Susan Wilson encourages the reader to believe and trust in her heart and in her higher instincts. Then it gives her some examples of how some very strong and successful women have used their hearts as well as their minds to learn and grow in their journey towards success."

—Mary Kramer, Iowa State Senator

"What a terrific book! Clear, thought-provoking, and very practical advice for any peak performer. I recommend it unreservedly."

—Nido Qubein, Chairman, Creative Services, Inc.
And Past President, National Speakers Association

"I applaud Susan Wilson for focusing on two of the most valuable assets that women bring to the workplace and to positions of leadership—our pragmatic intelligence and our nurturing nature. Another of our 'women things' is our propensity for sharing, which Susan's work elucidates beautifully. I enthusiastically recommend sharing this book with friends and loved ones of both sexes."

—Joy Corning, Lt. Governor of Iowa

To Doug, Reid, and Breanne who provide the loving challenge for using an intelligent heart consistently.

To Jean, a quiet and steady friend whose friendship is a jewel.

To the women who, with their intelligent hearts, have been important influences on my years of developing an intelligent heart:

Janet Large Hawkins
Nellie Large
Suzanne Arp Liberty, Ph.D.
Karen Hawkins Gillette
Sherry Holloway
Ann Swafford
Esther Balser
Cathy Job
Gail Flagel
Libby Whitaker
Gail Guge
Herberta Lundegren, Ph.D.
Karen Chapman
Susan Batterman

To the women who wish to live and love their lives more fully.

Contents

Acknowledgments

Although it took just a few months to write the first draft of the manuscript, the insights for *Your Intelligent Heart* evolved over time. In the past twelve years, hundreds of men and women contributed to this book by sharing their insights and experiences. I am grateful to them.

Many thanks go to Gary Kelly, a dear professional and personal friend, who has encouraged and supported me in many ways. I thank Gary, Suzanne Liberty, Karen Chapman, and David Geer for their review of the manuscript and for their valuable suggestions. Their encouragement has fueled my consulting and speaking career as well as my writing career. I am grateful to Andrea Pedolsky who was the first in the publishing world to tell me that I had writing talent and then spent hours getting it out of me. Memories of specific praise and encouragement from both Andrea and Mary Glenn, AMACOM editor for this book, are written on Post-its that I keep in my desk drawer. They continue to provide motivation for me. Beverly Miller also enhanced my manuscript with her excellent suggestions, and Associate Editor Barbara Horowitz of AMACOM lent her expertise as well.

I appreciate the focus group members—Jan Cooper, Katie Roth, Lori Hanson, Susan Wendel, Nancy Noth, Lynn Peterson, Amy Doerring, Gail Flagel, and Mollie Cooney—who contributed their insights and stories. And I thank Mary Andringa, Myrt Levin, Lieutenant Governor Joy Corning, and

Mary Kramer for their interviews. Additional thanks to Corine Hadley, who was willing to open the door for several of these valuable interviews.

Although it may come as a surprise to him, I am very grateful to Jim Autry. His living embraces the spirit of the intelligent heart. I met with him only a couple of times, but his warmth, his intellect, and his heart have meant much to me—really more than the written word can say.

The book was well underway but with a different title when I first saw the two words *intelligent heart* put together, in an article about Robert Barth, formerly the international president of Rotary. When I saw them, I knew they needed to be part of the title of this book. So I thank him for that inspiration.

I sincerely appreciate Vicki Wade, who helped with reviewing, proofing, and typing the manuscript. She provides valuable support, critique, and creativity to everything we undertake at Executive Strategies.

Eric Best seems to understand my passion for what I do; he helps me focus by his directed questions and provides invaluable suggestions. Thank you, Eric.

I am also grateful to members of the National Speakers Association whom I've met over the past three years. I have learned a great deal from you all, and I will continue to learn.

Finally, thank you, Doug, for supporting me with encouraging words and loving actions. You uphold a belief in my potential.

Your
INTELLIGENT
HEART

Introduction

STOP! Please take a moment to think. How do you feel about your life right now? Write your response to that question.

_____

_____

_____

    You may, by buying this book, change forever your way of thinking, behaving, and living. The concepts of this book are potentially so powerful that your way of embracing and experiencing your life may take you to a different level of existence.

    STOP again. Please take a moment to think. What are you contributing to this civilization? What is your gift to those with whom you work, live, and associate?

_____

_____

_____

    This is a book about unwrapping your heart—about finding out how wonderful it feels to work with and relate to others with love and not just because it is your responsibility. This is a book about developing your personal potential more fully than you ever imagined possible by taking your heart as well as your intellect into the workplace. There is unmatched value to building a consistent congruency between the loveliness and the strength of your heart and the intellect of your mind. *Your Intelligent Heart* provides a promise that life can be richer, fuller, and more colorful if we allow the strength of our hearts to connect with the strength of our minds.

This is a book to encourage you to seek your very best. Its ideas free you to contemplate, appreciate, and celebrate the calling of your own gifts and talents as well as those of others. Applying the ideas set out in this book will lead you to reach goals you hardly thought possible. You'll be more aware of investing your time and energy in meaningful action rather than in worrying, conflict, or fear. The strategies of this book will fill your internal treasure chest of insights and experiences.

The insights given here evolved as a result of my work with managers and executives over the past twelve years. Although my primary focus is to assist with management and interpersonal skills, I find that conversations often turn to issues of self-esteem and self-acceptance—issues that touch our hearts. People who learn to accept themselves, bruises, warts, and all, are much more effective as bosses and as leaders. They still hold themselves to high standards (many of which are in the book), but they also are accepting of their mistakes and their challenges to grow. As a result, they are more authentic and influential in their example to others—and they exude an aura of personal happiness and peace.

Choosing to read and use this book is a priceless gift to yourself. Developing your intelligent heart is a gift to yourself. Using your intelligent heart is a gift to all those with whom you interact. And over time, the impact of your intelligent heart will ripple over the lives of hundreds, maybe thousands, of others. With your intelligent heart, you will move mountains.

USING THIS BOOK

In reading *Your Intelligent Heart,* you will find 130-plus strategies for embracing the abundance of living. Too often we allow the urgency of the mundane and the trivial to get in the way, with our larger dreams shoved aside in the process. In allowing this, we may diminish the flame of belief in ourselves. If we consistently sacrifice ourselves for others' dreams, how can we build our own wholeness?

For a year, I worked with a woman as she struggled to become more comfortable with herself. We began meeting soon after she burst into tears following the inocuous question, "How are you?" For her, her reaction was a message to get some help. She wasn't sick, she wasn't out of control, but she was losing herself to others' demands and expectations. And the pressures were coming from friends, family, and the workplace. She is just one of many of us who, in this day and time, are seeking a more comfortable, self-accepting way of living.

Living.

We're tired of just going through the motions. But all of us need to embrace the loveliness and the responsibility of finding a richer way of life for ourselves. Developing an intelligent heart is a concept that has spoken to me. I first saw these words coupled by the former president of the Rotary International, Robert R. Barth. They jumped off the page to me. When I read them, I knew they embodied the concept that I've been working with for years in business. It is not enough to take intellectual prowess into the workplace. A personal warmth, a sense of true caring is also needed if we want to make a meaningful contribution to our world. It is in that caring and love for others that we take ourselves to a higher plane of living. In that caring and love for others, each of us is able to supersede self and provide service to others. And ironically, it is in heartfelt service to others that we show our very best selves.

The concept of the intelligent heart is not for women only, but in this book, the emphasis guides women to use specific ideas and strategies to embrace their lives, both professionally and personally, in a richer, more loving, and more gratifying way. The gentle, enduring strength of your intelligent heart is waiting for your attention.

Caring for Yourself
With an Intelligent Heart

Would you like to feel more confident? Is feeling capable important to you? Does loneliness overcome you now and then? If you answered yes to these questions, consider the health of your self-esteem. There is a lot of talk about self-esteem these days, and it's going on in and out of the workplace. But what about action? What can you *do* to feel better about yourself? Each of us wants to feel important and valuable. In developing your intelligent heart, you raise your capacity to feel valuable. As a result, you'll have more emotional room to value others—your employees, your colleagues, and even your boss. Most of the following suggestions for caring for yourself are practical and immediately applicable. Give yourself thirty days to see the results of your efforts. You will.

Establish a set of core values.

Know what is most important to you. Use your values as a beacon to establish your goals, make decisions, develop plans, and interact with others. Staying true to your beliefs helps you accomplish more with greater impact and less stress.

"I want to be me, I just want to be me," one of my clients cried plaintively. And when I asked, "Who are you?" she replied, "I don't know. I don't have enough room or time in my life to find out." The message is clear: It's difficult to be who you are if you haven't first established who or what you want to be. Knowing your values can help. By saying, "I believe in treating others with respect," "I believe in honest dealings more than profit," or "I believe that my family is more important than climbing the career ladder" you are providing information about who you are and what is important to you. Grab a pen and take notes throughout this book. On some pages you will find room to jot down your feelings or your own stories. Feel free to scribble in the margins. This is your book. Use it to record your own insights, emotions, and inspirations.

2

Establish a personal mission.

This is your personal philosophy that identifies what you believe and what you want to achieve in your life. Your values and the principles by which you live provide the foundation for your mission. Your immediate goals may change, but your mission is a constant to guide your effort.

These next questions are short, but they take some serious thought. Consider them, and write your responses. Why are you here? What do you intend to contribute before your death?

_____

_____

_____

3

Establish goals if results are important to you.

Without clearly established goals, many ideas remain dreams. In 1953, a survey was taken of the graduating class at Yale University with regard to the goals that class members set. Three percent of the graduating class responded with their goals for their lives. In their goal setting, this portion of the class considered what they intended to achieve and by when, resources to assist them with reaching their goals, obstacles to be overcome, a plan of action, and their motivation for achieving each goal. A follow-up study in 1973 found that the thirty-five who had written down their goals were worth more financially than the other 97 percent of their class.* The power of written goals!

*Virgis Colbert, "Successful Strategies for Achieving Your Career Goals," *Vital Speeches of the Day* (December 15, 1993).

$$\boxed{4}$$

Consider the long-term gains of attaining your goals rather than the short-term reward.

Many goals of truly worthy and life-enhancing value take time to achieve. Perhaps one of the disadvantages that we face in today's culture is that we already have too much. Our taste for immediate rewards is so great that we don't learn to appreciate the gift of the journey as we make progress toward worthy goals.

$$\boxed{5}$$

Claim your talents and skills.

Develop an understanding of the personal contribution that you make to your work—the contribution that goes beyond the technical skill. Reports, studies, and television talk shows claim that thousands are suffering from low self-esteem. Self-esteem goes up when people determine their talent and contribute that talent to society.

You can decide to contribute far more to your work than just your technical skill. Consider the different perspectives that two women bring to their organization. Part of Bonnie's responsibility is to correct errors by proofreading material. She takes pride in her work and relishes each opportunity to ensure error-free manuals. She sees herself as an essential asset to writers, and her enthusiasm for what she does buoys others. It is clear that Bonnie feels good about her contribution. For Joann, who also proofreads, the task is an annoyance. She makes it clear that proofreading is a burden and that she'll do it only until something better comes along. Rather than recognizing the contribution that her proofreading skill makes, she diminishes her personal value by consistently putting down her job.

6

Extend a helping hand to others.

Those confident enough to help others tend to exude confidence—a confidence that doesn't feel threatened by helping others move ahead. Your personal power is enhanced by your ability to serve others, and there is an added benefit of your willingness to help: "What goes around, comes around," so it is likely that the help you give will come back to you in your time of need.

Experts in leadership are finding that some of the strongest leaders are those who believe that, in serving others, they serve themselves. Businessman Earl Nightingale once said, "Pay attention to your contribution and your rewards will take care of themselves."

One of our challenges is to define our rewards. Too many of us define reward solely in terms of money. How about the rewards of building trust, others' faith in our leadership, an inner joy that we are doing the right thing? These are the rewards that endure.

7

Live your values.

Develop the courage to place your stake, and move it only when you believe that there is a compelling reason to do so. By living your values, you will develop a personal trustworthiness that others cannot share unless they too are living what they say they believe. For instance, if you value honesty, practice it every day in every circumstance to build your integrity about that value.

Lt. Governor of Iowa Joy Corning says, "I have some core values—honesty, fairness, and caring are a few—from which I am unwilling to waiver or compromise. Whether I am being a mother, or a teacher, or holding a public office, those core values guide my thoughts and actions. And I always ask myself, as I cautioned my children to ask themselves before taking action, 'Is it illegal, immoral, unhealthy, or unsafe?' "

8

Live your truths.

Living your truths builds your reservoir of personal power and influence. You create a synergy as you consistently and passionately adhere to your beliefs. Being true to yourself is more relevant than ever before as ideas, people, and situations pull at our time, our energy, and even our convictions. Honoring our truths helps us invest time and energy more wisely.

The CEO of a rehabilitation agency found herself more and more at odds with a key union representative as negotiations approached. A contentious issue was that of self-directed work teams. The union representative viewed them as union busting; the CEO was implementing them to empower all employees and to serve their customers better. Although the CEO, who disliked conflict, had to deal with several rude confrontations with this person, she stood by her conviction that the teams were useful and important to the future of the agency. Over time, her calm consistency about her beliefs through her words, actions, and behaviors influenced the majority of employees, even those who had initially been supporters of the union representative's point of view.

9

Advise with caution.

Even when you are certain that your advice is sound and your intent pure, be aware that the receiver of your advice may not want it. In order for your advice to be truly helpful, the recipient must desire it and have the potential for using it.

As a management consultant, I was once counseled in the following way when in the midst of offering my opinion that wasn't asked for: "Susan, has it ever occurred to you that people don't want your advice unless they are paying for it?" And the message, though blunt, was useful. Advice, no matter how potentially useful, is wasted if the recipient is not prepared to receive it. Advice is only as helpful as the receiver wants it to be.

10

Face up to situations, even painful ones.

Your ability to confront issues and to admit your part in them builds others' trust in you. Regardless of position or status, being perceived as trustworthy is a strong and desirable asset. The ability to say, "I am sorry," "I made a mistake," or "I wish that I had handled things differently" is far more impressive than the pursuit of perfection. Others intuitively know that perfection is elusive, so admitting wrongs is honest and caring. Instead of trying to convince others of your rightness, invest that time and energy into fixing or resolving the error. Your value to others doesn't depend on your being right; rather, its roots are in your integrity.

An emergency room physician lost her temper with an attending nurse while caring for a small child. After the child was taken care of, the doctor approached the nurse and apologized for her behavior. What was impressive to the nurse and of interest to observers was that the physician recognized and apologized for the loss of her temper. The nurse remembered, "When she apologized, I admired her more for her willingness to admit her wrong than I've ever admired her technical skills. If she can apologize, than she is more human than I realized."

11

Avoid focusing on problems. Solve them or turn them into opportunities.

Too often, viewing a challenge as a problem leads to a negative mind-set that diminishes your personal power and influence. Viewing a challenge as an opportunity embraces the concept that there is more from which to learn and grow.

> "I need problems. A good problem makes me come alive."
>
> —Tiny Roland, CEO of Lonrho

David Geer, a friend in the ministry, sees focusing on problems as rooted in a "reforming vision"—that is, making better what is. We sometimes need to let go of what is in order to free our thinking to create something new.

12

You made a mistake? Focus on what you can learn from it, and move on.

An executive who works in the temporary personnel industry shares this thought: "I try to keep mistakes of employees and even my own in perspective. Over the years, I've discovered that just about anything can be fixed." The owner of a physical and occupational rehabilitation business adds, "You know,

I've found that mistakes plus the passing of time equals an improved sense of humor. And in working with people, I surely do need my sense of humor!"

13

Plan to avoid needless problems.

Problems frequently arise because of a lack of planning. Answer the questions of who, what, where, when, how, and why, and you've designed a blueprint for success.

A consultant once provided the secret to her high proposal acceptance rate. In writing her proposals, she provides information about the specific project (what), participants (who), location (where), date and time (when), objectives (why), and the program schedule (how), and thus she increases the probability of others' understanding and accepting her ideas. As a result, clients see in her confidence that she is knowledgeable, thorough, and prepared to take action.

14

Reduce the potential for a problem even further by considering what can go wrong with your plan.

If you identify a potential problem, decide on the actions for preventing it or for minimizing its effects. After investing time to plan carefully, it may seem redundant to some to look for problems. But identifying potential problems can be the catalyst for making your plan more successful.

In preparation for a meeting, a presenter had outlined a plan with steps that clearly stated who was to do what by when. When reviewing her plan, she discovered a potential problem with the printer's meeting her deadline, and meeting this deadline affected the next step in her plan. Her solution was to get a written commitment from the printer that the work would be done on time. She also decided to get the materials to him earlier so that he would have more time within which to work. These two actions helped reduce the probability of a missed deadline.

$$\boxed{15}$$

Thoughtfully review your plans; it reduces stress and distress. And your planning shows a respect and courtesy toward the time, energy, and resources of others.

When there is a lack of planning, lower productivity, poorer quality of work, confusion and disorganization, higher costs, and greater pressure may result. Lack of planning is expensive financially, emotionally, and physically.

"My lack of planning will not become your crisis" is a perspective to remember. Front-line supervisors in a paper mill complained that they often had too many crises on their hands. A conversation with their boss revealed that there was little time spent in planning. Once their boss made a commitment to do a better job of planning tasks, resources, and responsibilities, the crews saw a drop in the number of crises because they had a plan for handling situations as they arose.

16

Establish your priorities. Then make room for them.

In this way, you will keep focused on the results that you want to achieve.

Myrt Levin, director of the Iowa Business Council, says: "Know what you are in your job to do. Knowing your mission, knowing your goals helps you to push the unnecessary stuff aside. We don't have time to focus on anything other than what we need to do to get the job done."

17

Conduct a quarterly performance review—on yourself!

Are you living your values? Making progress toward your goals? Are there behaviors that you need to change to be more effective? Are your priorities what you want them to be? Use a standard performance evaluation, make one up, or consider asking employees for input, but select a systematic method for reviewing your progress. The results will provide information that helps you determine your path toward personal success.

People often can create their own circumstances and luck. What about you? Specifically, what changes can you make to create more of your own "luck"?

_____

_____

_____

18

Determine if your life is paying the dividends that you want.

Are you reducing stressful ways of living? Do you like what you are doing? Do you like yourself? Answering these kinds of questions helps you make this determination. You have the freedom and the capability to be the architect of your life. Design, build, paint your life as you want it to be. Embrace yourself with a loving spirit.

> "The cities and mansions that people dream of are those in which they finally live."
>
> —Lewis Mumford

19

Maintain a sense of humor.

Life is serious, but avoid taking yourself too seriously. Look for life's laugh lines. They can be found nearly anywhere . . .

when you start looking. People who can laugh at themselves often have a wit and candor that is refreshment to others. Smile. Chuckle. Laugh out loud. You can't? Then try again. Smile. Chuckle. Laugh out loud. Your personal appeal is enhanced by a sense of humor. And laughter may make life better and longer.

The person who has a sense of humor may not be a leader, but an effective leader must have a sense of humor.

20

Always remember that you are capable of changing in ways that are important to you.

The old saying, "You can't teach an old dog new tricks," doesn't apply to humans. And your changes often mean vast improvement to your life.

> "Sometimes a life, like a house, needs renovating, the smell of new wood, new rooms in the heart, unimagined until one begins the work. One rebuilds because the structure deserves a renewing."
> —Doris Schwerin

21

Avoid naysayers.

Flee from others' fears and negativism. Many naysayers defend their negative views by saying that their views are "reality," but remember that reality is in the eyes of the beholder. So tell others to stop raining on your parade. Create your own weather for your life.

Mary Andringa, president of Vermeer Manufacturing, in Pella, Iowa, made this observation: "If you come up against folks who only see the negative, move away from them to those who encourage and challenge you. I think that it's important to cultivate an accepting attitude toward others, but if someone or something is not good for you, then take the personal responsibility to make the choice that improves your situation."

22

Live today.

Living in the past is a waste of your precious and limited resources of time and energy. Time and energy applied to the past is time and energy taken away from the present. Apply your resources to make progress toward your goals.

Too many of us squander time living our lives from the rear-view mirror. We ask ourselves, "What should have been? What might have been? If only I had . . ." This hopeless meandering steals your time and energy. If you feel the need to worry or live in the past, do so for a specific amount of time each week and then STOP. Redirect your precious time and energy to actions that help you make progress toward your goals.

A letter to Ann Landers became a favorite of mine because of her response. The writer talked of being older and of wanting to return to medical school and of being eight years older before getting the medical degree. Ann Landers replied, "And how old will you be if you don't go back to school?" Many, many people, in reflecting about the past, emphasize how important it is to have a dream *and* to follow it—not for money, not for prestige, not for someone else's dream, but for yourself. A piece of you withers and dies if you do not.

23

Live an example.

How often have you heard, "Do as I say, not as I do"? And isn't it true that our most memorable examples are those people who lived their beliefs as opposed to just talking about them?

A woman who was a fourth-grade teacher died two years ago. During her two-year illness, she heard from dozens of people—students, colleagues, parents of students, former students, their parents, friends, acquaintances, even the president of Duke University—and the common theme in their communication was how Janet had touched their lives. She had made learning exciting and also was a living example of caring and self-improvement. She greeted each day with the goal of being just a little bit better than the day before.

24

Strive for high standards, but don't try to be perfect.

The first thought is a motivator, the second is a bore. Perfectionism is a game with no winner. Standards of perfection are not grounded in reality.

A colleague who was trying to change some perfectionistic tendencies made this observation: "When I try to be perfect, I realize that I begin to focus on myself rather than on the task to be done. I spin my wheels trying to get it better and better and better until I feel like a whirling dervish, similar to a skater going into a spin that gets faster and faster. And while I get so intense about me, I lose my focus on the important bigger picture." Striving to be better and better is an investment of time and energy; trying to be perfect is a waste of those resources.

25

Know that you are lovable and capable but that the meanings are mutually exclusive.

Too often, we feel needy in terms of our ability to enjoy meaningful relationships. We're so busy doing and accomplishing that we confuse the difference between being accepted for who we are and being appreciated for what we contribute.

Some women believe that if only they could accomplish

more, they would earn people's love. They measure their capacity for being lovable by their ability to achieve. A recently divorced friend told me wistfully, "I thought I was doing the right thing to put a lot of hours in at work so that my husband would be proud of me and would appreciate my income. But his pride in me did not make him love me more."

26

Believe in yourself.

Most of us experience days when this is difficult. However, building a track record of believing in yourself develops a quiet self-confidence that shows itself in your daily living. The resulting calm and poise pays dividends to your work and relationships.

Several years ago, some coworkers agreed to try a pity party when the going got rough. The invitation to a pity party is simple. Most often, it is private—just the person who needs to indulge in self-pity is invited—and brief—only ten or fifteen minutes. Ranting, raving, crying, and blaming are allowed. Then the party is over. Finished. And the victim turns into victor as her time and energy are channeled to figuring out solutions or alternatives to the current dilemma. Although a pity party may not work for everyone, for many it's been a creative outlet for tears and frustrations. Then the focus on solving problems builds a quiet confidence that leads to an inner calm.

> "Self-esteem isn't everything; it's just that there's nothing without it."
>
> —Gloria Steinem

27

Accept praise gracefully.

Some of us are genuinely uncomfortable receiving praise. If you are, try smiling and saying, "Thank you" when you receive a compliment. As you become more comfortable with accepting kind words, offer a bit more of yourself, which can make the giver of praise feel good too: "Thank you, I appreciate your noticing the detail that went into this meeting. Your comments make my day."

The ability to accept praise gracefully sends a message about healthy self-esteem. Most of us deserve regular and sincere praise. You deserve to like and appreciate yourself. In working with an executive who has done a remarkable job of saving a business, I found that she was overly self-effacing about her success. She showed her discomfort with praise by hanging her head to the side, avoiding eye contact, and quickly moving on to other topics. Instead of sending a message of humility, her behavior was perceived as lacking confidence and poise—not advantageous in an executive position.

28

Allow others to do for you.

Some of us are so busy helping others that sometimes it is difficult to be the recipient of kind deeds. But others want to make a contribution too. Let them. Your willingness to allow others to help you balances the power between you and others.

A senior-level executive shared this anecdote: "One of the nicest compliments that I've ever received was from a front-line employee who told me that even though I was the CEO, I was just 'regular.' When I asked what she meant, she said, 'Well you let others do things for you and for this company; and you tell us thank you instead of ignoring it or taking the credit for it.'"

┌─────────┐
│   29   │
└─────────┘

Respect your anger, but consider it carefully before taking action.

Of course we get angry; it is part of our passion about the way that we feel. But anger is a feeling—neither bad nor good until we make a choice about how to express it. Give yourself time to think through the situation that has aroused your anger so that you can respond rationally, respectfully, and with dignity.

While serving on a hospital board, I had the opportunity to work with its president who taught me a powerful lesson about anger. His anger was over an issue with the medical staff. Prior to meeting with them, he made his decisions about how angry he was, how he would express his anger, and how he would conduct himself. During the meeting with representative members of the medical group, he remained in control of his behavior throughout, but his planned words and actions communicated a strong sense of presence about his opinions and plans for resolution of the problem. In spite of the losses of temper on the part of several other people, the president remained in control of the meeting, treated all with respect, and maintained his composure.

30

Understand your anger.

Often the feeling of anger is a mask for a more vulnerable feeling—perhaps hurt, frustration, disappointment, or insecurity. These more vulnerable feelings often occur because a goal has been derailed.

About ten of a group of thirty salespeople, meeting for a quarterly conference, were expressing their anger about a new performance appraisal system and a new compensation system. The discussion was loud, verbal, and increasingly aggressive. Then the question was raised: Why are you feeling so angry? One by one, participants admitted feelings of hurt, humiliation, and a sense of feeling devalued by their company. As each spoke, the air of tension lessened. And as the group began to use their energy for problem solving rather than for their anger, their personal control over their choices gained strength. The result was a plan for asking senior management to be better communicators about changes, as well as a plan for improving the sales performance of this group.

31

Your life and how you think about it is yours and yours alone.

Others understand you only to the extent that you effectively communicate your reality. Conversely, avoid presuming that you can understand someone else until that person has had a chance to communicate his or her perspective to you.

> "People have one thing in common: They are all different."
>
> —Robert Zend

32

Take care of yourself—your intellectual and emotional self as well as your physical self.

Your overall well-being is a merging of these three areas. Treating each part of yourself in healthy ways allows a richness of living that isn't possible when a part of you is sick or unhealthy. Actively seeking ways to care for yourself—your whole self—is a wellness lifestyle. People who practice this lifestyle are stronger, more confident, and healthier in nearly every way.

Consider your goals and your lifestyle. What three specific changes could you make for the next thirty days that would lead to healthier living?

_____

_____

_____

33

Give up the goal of having it "all."

Probably none of us can have it "all." Choosing one thing means *not* choosing something else. Choosing one goal means giving up some others. Instead of trying to have it "all," consider the value of getting "a lot." Healthy living, effective goal setting, and improving personal effectiveness contribute to maximizing your contentment.

A friend who was driving to work one day remembers a radio interview with Meryl Streep, mother, wife, and actress. She recounted the story by telling us that the interviewer had asked Meryl Streep this question: "Katherine Hepburn has been quoted as saying that she didn't marry and have children because if you want to work, you can't have it all. Do you agree with her?" Ms. Streep thought a moment and replied, "Was I late for this interview?" Surprised, the interviewer responded, "As a matter of fact, you were about ten minutes late." Then Ms. Streep said, "Well, I think that you can have it all if you're willing to be about ten minutes late."

The point is, you can do what you want if you're willing to give up something to get something. You can't have it "all," but you can make choices to optimize your joy in living.

34

Consider whether you really want it "all."

Having it "all" means more time and energy expended to get it, take care of it, use it, fix it, and store it, until you decide to sell it or give it away! Doesn't that sound as though "it" is owning *you,* instead of vice versa? How about applying that time and energy to making the most of appreciating what you do have and pursuing your most meaningful goals!

What are you willing to stop doing in order to have more time and energy to invest in what is most important to you?

_____

_____

_____

35

You are responsible for your own happiness.

It is important to learn about what makes you happiest so that you can make the choices that yield the results you want. One woman shares this story: "My mother wore the same red dress to church for years because the important thing to her was to save enough money to put her three children through college. I asked her if she wouldn't like a new dress, if that would make her happy. And she told me that her happiness was knowing her long-term goals for her family and working to make them come true. A new church dress was not part of that picture."

36

You are not responsible for another's happiness—no matter how hard he or she tries to tell you that you are.

Part of maturing is recognizing that you are responsible and accountable for your own choices and recognizing that others have that same responsibility and freedom in their lives.

Let your personal freedom ring by taking the responsibility for your choices. Denis Waitley, author and motivational speaker, suggests that there needs to be a Statue of Responsibility standing next to the Statue of Liberty. We enrich each other by our relationships, but each of us is responsible for our own happiness.

37

Really wanting something makes a difference in how hard you try to get it.

Instead of idly wishing for many things, decide what it is that you really want. Then consider what motivates you to get it. Be specific. Concentrate on those things that are important to you so that you can set goals and establish a plan for reaching them. Dedicating your time and energy to a step-by-step plan raises the probability that you will achieve what you most desire.

Results in life generally don't just happen. Even the

"overnight successes" frequently have spent years in trying to perfect their craft through persistence, perspiration, and dedication to hard work. They find that their rewards depend on the quality and amount of time and energy that they contribute to their goals.

38

Want something badly enough to work hard for it.

The process you will go through builds character and skills. For many of us, not achieving something is more a matter of "I won't do it" than "I can't do it." Get the difference? With "I can't," you tell yourself that you don't have a choice. With "I won't," you are recognizing that you do have the power of choice. It's a subtle but powerful message that we give ourselves. Isn't it time to focus on: I can because I choose to?

39

Confront your fears.

If you don't, they may loom even larger. Confronting and overcoming debilitating fears builds your confidence for resolving problems and contributes to your self-esteem and the poise that you exude. Eliminating fear also means that you have additional time and energy to apply to getting results.

There are steps to confronting your fears. Try answering these questions:

What is one of your fears that is inhibiting progress toward one of your goals?

What is the worst that could happen? (Often the worst is not that bad.)

What is the probability of having the worst occur?

What can you do to reduce or eliminate this fear?

On a separate sheet of paper, consider a plan of action. Remember to answer the questions who, what, when, where, how, and why.

40

Behave as if you have courage.

Chances are, you will. So discipline yourself to walk purposefully and with your chin up. You will get results. To paraphrase Mark Twain, courage is resistance to fear, not absence of fear.

The *Book of Lists* claims that the fear of speaking is the number one fear of many. But for our work, for our community, perhaps even for our family, we find that we have to speak up. People who have shared their fear of speaking say that their strategy for overcoming it was simply to convince themselves that they could do it and that they would do it.

41

Choices: Learn to love yours.

Make informed choices in terms of your goals, relationships, and daily living. Opening one door means closing others, but the door you open leads to other choices. Instead of investing your personal resources wishing for what might have been, invest that energy and time in making the best of your current choices.

A respected attorney who worked in the corporate setting vacillated about whether to continue her work with the corporation or step out to open a private practice. Gradually her productivity, as well as her personal happiness, declined. She felt trapped and leery of moving in any direction. Once she made the choice to stay with her firm, she felt a new sense of freedom and renewed enthusiasm to dedicate herself to her work. Closing the door on a different career choice (for now!) freed her time and energy for her corporate work.

42

Save and savor the "atta girls."

You probably deserve more praise than you get, but save and savor what you do receive. When you are having a blue day, rereading those letters or remembering kind words lifts morale and will inspire your continued effort.

A friend of mine actually has a manila file she labeled "Attagirls." She knows from experience that its notes lift her perspective, her energy, and her willpower. Their impact actually raises her vision of herself. Sometimes she has "bad moments" but rarely a "bad day."

43

Believe in something greater than yourself.

Develop your faith, love your faith, live your faith. Great leaders, in living their faith, communicate more clearly through their example than their words.

Believing in something greater than yourself keeps you going. You go on for the bigger picture, for the vision, for the greater plan rather than just for yourself. A question that helps me to keep the perspective that I want is, "What is the best use of my time and energy to glorify God?" The question reminds me of my reason for being.

Caring for Others With an Intelligent Heart

"No one cares how much you know, until they know how much you care" is a statement that I've heard frequently in recent years as people emphasize the importance of loving one another. There are myriad ideas for demonstrating to others that you care for them. Caring needs to be a part of most interactions—at work, at home, at play, and in service to others. Most of us don't lie on our deathbeds wishing that we had accomplished more tasks, but frequently we wish for repaired relationships. Do something about relationships now. How do you honor those in your work life as well as in your personal life? Do you value others with an "ahhh," or do you treat them with an "ugh"?!! Card companies suggest saying it with cards, and florists want you to say it with flowers. How do you say, "I care about you"? You can provide consistent messages of "I care" through your voice, your posture, and your thoughts, as well as through your actions. Use the proven ideas in this section, and you give more heart to your relationships.

44

Consider the value of "nice."

A lot of women are tired of the idea of being nice, but what's so great about the alternative? You can operate from a position of strength and power and still be nice. In my experience with both men and women over the years, those who treat others well end up with far more personal power and influence than those who do not because they've taken care to respect the needs of others. Being nice, even when you don't have to, is worth the effort.

There is a resort in Phoenix that has a coffee bar near its front entrance. On my way out, I purchased a coffee drink and gave the employee a card to charge it to my room. JoAnn handed it back to me, and said, "I'm sorry, but we only take cash." And then she added, with a smile, "Don't worry about it; just bring the money later." I expressed my concern about possibly forgetting to return. Still smiling and sincere, JoAnn said, "Then consider it a gift." What a lift. What a gift. The true gift was not the cappuccino if I did forget to pay for it but her choosing to treat me in a nice way that respected me as a person. She treated me with an "ahhh"! Her respect and kindness not only influenced my decision to go get the money right then but also resulted in a personal note to the hotel about her level of customer service.

> "Being considerate of others will take you and your children further in life than any college or professional degree."
>
> —Marian Wright Edelman

45

Avoid gossip.

When you spend time and energy gossiping, you have less time and energy to apply to reaching your goals and living your values. With gossip, feelings are hurt, communication is more complicated, and relationships often are irreparably damaged. That's a lot of pain for allowing loose lips.

I've found that when communication is on the up-and-up, I don't worry nearly as much about what others are saying about me. As a result, communication is honest and more relaxed, and I enjoy richer relationships.

46

If you can't say something nice, don't say anything at all.

Our mothers had it right: It is better to say nothing than to say something hurtful and risk damaging the self-esteem of someone else. Many would rather be wounded with a fist than with words. Physical bruises heal. Why is it that so many people justify hurtful words by saying that they are just being honest? Honesty without the support of respect often equates to mean-spirited words.

A business friend was asked, "Why are you so positive? How do you stay up so much of the time?" Her first response was, "I don't know." But after reflection, she continued, "I've become that way over the years by looking for and accepting the good in myself, which has given me the freedom to look for and affirm the good in others. And I choose to see, hear, and talk about ideas that are uplifting rather than deflating."

Please listen.

People are desperate to be heard. In fact, many pay money to have someone listen to them. In our culture, listening is one of the ways that we demonstrate respect for someone else, yet how often do we offer that respect? How often do we say we are listening when actually we are concentrating on something else? How often do we allow our conversations to be interrupted? Listen carefully and responsively. It is a gift that you give.

A manager recently called me and suggested that, in working with companies, I focus on listening as a highly valued skill to be developed. She went on to identify the costs associated with poor listening: mistakes, rework, conflicts, misunderstood directions, and lower self-esteem of employees. Her view is that an investment in listening carefully and responsively is an investment in the healthy futures of companies.

48

Be flexible to others' points of view.

Rarely are opinions absolute. There are many shades of gray. Accepting different points of view even on those subjects that you feel expert demonstrates confidence. Often it is the insecure who feel a need to hold on to only one point of view.

At Bloomingdale's some years ago, the woman who designed and arranged the displays was working with some mannequins and didn't like the position of their arms. So she broke them off and taped them back to positions that were more effective for her display. Flexibility—the ability to break off from one perspective to see things from a different point of view—is an enriching personal quality to develop.

Frequently groups of employees establish guidelines for their behavior when meeting together. Inevitably, regardless of the kind of company, the level of employee, or the purpose of the group, members of the group agree that listening to one another and remaining open-minded to different points of view are critical guidelines for the success of their meetings.

49

Invite employee input and respond to it.

Employees would rather not give input at all than to give it and not have a response. From their perspective, a lack of response suggests a lack of caring.

Top executives in one travel agency invite employees to spend half a day with them on a regular basis. They find that not only do employees benefit from learning more about their leaders' roles, but these executives build in the opportunity to listen to the employee with whom they work for that half-day. They listen to employee needs, concerns, and ideas.

50

Strive to be consistently open and honest in your communication.

We are all so different that it is difficult to communicate clearly even in the best of circumstances. When we choose to withhold information, gossip, stretch the truth, or overreact, we pave the way for a collision in communications.

Write down two examples of communication skills that you need to improve. Be specific. When do they occur? With whom? Where? Why? And what are they about? (For example, "In my job, I delegate to employees without giving them the information that they need to get the job done.")

_____

_____

_____

Now decide what you are willing to do to change your behavior. Answer these questions as you identify a communication strategy. Who will do what by when? (For example, "When delegating to employees, I will ask, 'What additional information do you need from me?'")

_____

_____

_____

51

Develop a positive framework of thought.

Rarely are life's circumstances all bad. We tend to "sow what we reap." We also tend to sow what we read, think, discuss, and practice through our actions. If we strive for a consistently positive outlook on those things that we do, we can expect to reap positive results. Patience often is needed, but positive results are guaranteed.

A bonus here is that a positive perspective tends to raise our beliefs about our personal standards, opportunities, and possibilities. So not only do we reap more positive results as a result of our positive planting, but those results are of a higher level and quality.

52

Offer to help just because it is the right thing to do.

Choose to do nice things each day through courtesies, through gifts of time, energy, and conversation, and through looking for what needs to be done.

In finding ways to serve others, you serve yourself. Remember the idea of sowing what you reap? Look for ways to help others three, four, maybe even five times each day. Assist with no thought of a payback. It's a habit that pays dividends in terms of how you appreciate the humanity of others as well as yourself.

53

Learn and use good manners.

Good manners show an understanding of treating others with dignity and respect. The manner of your manners matters. "Thank you." "Please." "Excuse me." "May I help you?" These bywords of effective customer service should extend to employees as well. If we want employees to honor customers with good manners, we need to honor employees in the same way. Dozens of employees, when asked how they would like appreciation shown to them, have responded, "Just tell me 'thank you' when I do a good job. I just wish that someone would thank me."

"Courtesy—it is the mark of civilization."

—David Geer

54

Avoid using absolutes.

Rarely are words like *totally, always, never, absolutely, completely,* or *inevitably* the basis for a true statement, and your listeners intuitively know this. Using absolutes creates a barrier in communication.

Not too long ago when I was working with an employee team, I kept hearing phrases such as, "You're always on my back," "You never include me," and "You're absolutely wrong." When I asked those listening how they felt about those comments, they said, "That kind of language makes me feel defensive because deep down I know that the truth is not being spoken when others use absolute words. So then I wonder what else that person is saying that isn't quite true."

| 55 |

Learn the definition of assertion.

It is not related to the term *aggression,* as is often assumed. Assertion is an open and honest behavior style that expects to be treated with dignity and respect and that treats others in the same manner.

Often people use the terms *aggressive* and *assertive* in the same breath. Although both forms of communication are thought to offer honesty, there are two key differences. One is that assertive communication offers mutual respect. The other is that assertive communicators listen carefully and responsively, an outward sign of their respect for others. Sadly, an aggressive style does neither.

| 56 |

Be willing to say no when you feel that you must.

There is a limit to what each of us can give. When you don't establish your limits, others may take advantage of you. Express your perspective respectfully but honestly. It's okay to say no. In fact, for the health of communication, it's essential. If you don't learn to say no, you imply to others that it is all right to make demands on your energy and your time. Assert yourself by deciding who, where, when, and how much to give.

The preschool teacher of a friend's daughter called her to make cookies for a school party. As a full-time working mom, she already felt stretched in terms of her time and energy, but she also wanted to help in some way. After quickly assessing her alternatives, she offered to donate money so that cookies could be purchased at a local backery. She thus satisfied her need to contribute while avoiding any further stress on the use of her time and energy.

57

When you make a commitment, follow up and follow through, even when it is difficult.

In doing so, you raise your credibility. So many people fall short of their commitments that others are impressed when you consistently do what you say you will. Remember that in making a commitment, you are setting a goal. It may be made up of five steps or fifty steps, but persist with the perspiration and dedication required to honor your commitment.

Judy was called by a trusted friend and colleague who told her that he had recommended her as a candidate for assisting a national fraternity with its change in vision and strategic direction. Thrilled, she asked him what skills prompted his recommendation since she had no prior experience with either fraternities or sororities. His reply? "You set goals well, you persist despite formidable obstacles, and you consistently follow through."

58

To really make an impact, don't meet expectations. Exceed them!

Underpromise and overdeliver. Surprise by surpassing what you promise, and you will build a reputation for consistency and high quality. We are so used to hearing people overpromise and underdeliver that we sit up and take notice of the person who does the opposite.

A recent study examining the aggravations that people experience in conducting business identified the biggest gripe as people not following through on their commitments. Keeping your commitments communicates integrity, respect for the parties involved, and an appreciation for the business relationship. Remember that it is just as important to keep commitments to employees as to customers.

59

Write thank-you notes.

As a rule, people hear plenty of criticism and take a number of lumps through the day but don't hear when things are going right. Take the time to write a note that says what you appreciate in a specific and sincere way. Words are nice, but notes often are saved for days when a pick-me-up is needed.

An executive in the ministry has a file of personal notes from others. So does the president of a manufacturing company and the CEO of a rehabilitation facility. Many people I know save those personal notes. These files that many of us keep contain letters, notes, and cards that tug at our hearts because they are personal thanks for relationships and partnerships in business. The sincere, specific appreciation expressed is a motivation to continually surpass expectations. These notes and letters also provide moments to think about how our lives count in seemingly small matters as well as major achievements.

60

Assume the best in a situation.

Frequently people live through the day believing that the bad things that happen, the unhappy communications, and the frustrating situations are a result of someone who is out to get them. Rarely is this true. When instead you assume the best, you raise the probability of resolving the frustrations of a day.

Actively pursue the best in someone else and in yourself. Instead of retreating when you hear a cutting comment or a scathing criticism, look the sender of the message directly in the eye and ask, "What do you mean by that?" or "Why do you feel that way?" or "Why are you saying that?" Maintain your assertive stance of mutually respectful behavior. No one puts you down or ruins your day without your permission, so refuse to give it. Instead, insist that the situation or the conversation be raised to a higher level.

61

Be the first to extend a word or a handshake of welcome.

Newcomers often feel awkward and out of place because no one has taken a moment to greet them. Open your circle with a smile, turning to include the newcomer, or walking over to introduce yourself. Find a way to invite yourself into that new person's life.

When I was growing up, my mother kept a timeless quote on our refrigerator door. Others came and went, but this one stayed until it was yellowed with age. The words remain fresh and true: "The person with the greatest amount of class in a room is the person who makes the least number of people feel uncomfortable." As the president of a realty company said, "You can't go wrong finding a way to care about someone else regardless of the situation."

62

Shy behavior is sometimes selfish behavior.

If you realize that you are feeling awkward or lonely, perhaps you need to quit thinking about your feelings and extend a hand to someone else in the room. Concern for another is a quick cure to feeling out of place. My mother shared this wisdom with me when I was in fifth grade, and I've never forgotten it. She was right. Each time I make an effort to help someone else feel more comfortable, my discomfort fades.

A businesswoman who runs a heavy equipment manufacturing plant is memorable in her approach to others. When greeting guests and employees, she smiles warmly, gives a firm handshake, and asks, "How are *you?*" What a great start to a meeting with her!

63

Appreciate others.

This seems to be one of the most underutilized activities in the business world. We all thirst for appreciation for a job well done. And we'll tell you so if you take the time to ask!

An older middle manager in an aluminum rolling mill heard this statement and growled, "Well, my employees know they are doing a good job if I'm not on their backs," And within a second, one of his workers shot back, "Oh, no we don't." Praise. It's a desirable commodity.

64

It's worth saying again: Motivate others by appreciating them.

A Japanese proverb says, "One kind word can warm three winter months." Kind actions have impact as well.

Nine self-directed work teams arrived for a training session. Paula, one of the team leaders, brought fresh flowers in a vase and set them on the metal table. What a lovely sight that was. And team members were pleasantly surprised.

What compliments have kept you fueled and fired up?

_____

_____

_____

"If you don't show your appreciation to your people, then they will stop caring, and if they stop caring, you will find yourself out of business."

—LuAnn Sullivan, Wells Fargo Bank
branch manager

65

Ask employees what is important to them.

They know—and generally they want to tell you. All you need to do is ask the question. And you'll discover that their ideas often cost little to nothing to implement.

A group of employees was asked to brainstorm ways that appreciation could be shown to them. After identifying a number of ideas and prioritizing the top ones, they provided this list: treat us fairly, provide both positive and negative feedback, develop camaraderie, communicate openly and honestly, listen to us, and say thank you.

66

When a misunderstanding occurs between you and another person, shoulder your share of the blame.

You reduce defensiveness and strengthen the probability of improved communication when you admit your part of the misunderstanding.

One of the most effective questions to ask when preparing to resolve a conflict is, "What can I do for you?" And if an apology is warranted, make one. State it clearly, specifically, and respectfully.

Employees on a rehabilitation work team tried this and then reported its effectiveness. One of them said, "I'm usually pretty defensive when someone criticizes me. But this time, I calmly asked what I could do for this other person. After she got over her shock, she told me. And her response gave us a basis for some calm discussion."

67

Smile.

A smile from you often generates a smile from others. It is a small investment that pays large dividends in goodwill and good feelings. In our culture, smiling is a way of reaching out to others. Would it be worth it to you to smile more frequently if you knew that you were building better relationships?

Several managers were discussing their gripes about their plant manager. One of their strongest complaints had to do with her lack of smiling and saying hello when passing people in the halls. It may sound like a small issue, but as soon as this plant manager changed her behavior, perceptions about her friendliness changed and had a positive impact on working relationships.

68

Use people's names.

It's one more way to show respect and appreciation to others. Take an informal survey of how frequently you hear people's names used. You may be surprised. It's remarkable how infrequently some people call others by name, yet each of us likes the sound of our name. Be a name caller!

A colleague in the Northeast was known throughout New York State (or so it seemed!) for his ability to hear names once and remember them. And he also could hear information about an employee's family and be able to recall it— sometimes years later. In one instance, after having met a man two years before at a training seminar, Dick saw him at a gas station in Albany, New York. Without missing a beat, Dick called him by name and asked questions about this man's wife and daughter. What a way to make someone's day!!

69

Be accepting.

Each of us has unique qualities and gifts that make us delightfully different from each other. Appreciating the differences rather than criticizing them contributes to our inner calm, as well as to the way we get along with others.

Go a step further: *Celebrate* the differences among people. It's a worthy use of your time and energy. Some of the healthiest companies are those that celebrate people's differences. Of course, those differences must come together to work for the good of the company, but we can celebrate the wonder of differences. A bonus is that you make people feel special. And similar to what author Jim Autry says in *Love and Profit,* everybody deserves special treatment.

70

Care enough about a relationship to be honest—even when it hurts.

Honesty within the context of love and respect hurts less than an untruth when all is discovered, said, and done.

Frequently we defend our lack of honesty in relationships by murmuring that we don't want to hurt anyone's feelings or lower someone's morale. But over and over again, employees have told me that they want to hear criticism if it is fair, specific, and given in private. They are even more willing to hear it if they also believe that they are praised for the good work that they do. Employees express strong dislike for criticism that arrives through the grapevine, only at performance appraisal time, or in front of others.

$$\boxed{71}$$

When in conversation, look for the topic in common.

People are more comfortable if they believe they share common interests, values, or perspectives. Talented conversationalists suggest asking questions to determine areas of commonality that can spark a more caring and insightful conversation.

Prepare yourself for gatherings by developing some interesting, specific questions that are relevant to the event. Dan Krumm, the former CEO and chairman of the board of Maytag Corporation, was at a Christmas gathering of about thirty people who represented several levels at the corporation. He approached a group of five women (three of them secretaries) with a relaxed smile, an outstretched hand, and said, "Hello, my name is Dan Krumm." After completing introductions, he initiated a conversation by mentioning the dollhouse that he had built for his granddaughter. Right away, these women felt at ease. Several had granddaughters, they had owned dollhouses in their youth, and so instead of feeling awkward with the chairman of the board, they fell into easy conversation with him.

72

Give. Give your time, your talent, and your money.

Some people suggest "giving until it hurts." Interestingly, there is so much satisfaction in compassionate giving that the hurt is hardly noticeable, if there at all. So perhaps a goal is to give until it feels good!

Giving. Another way to serve others that comes back to bless us as well. There are dozens of ways to give. Take a treat to the office unexpectedly. Write a note to a child's teacher. Hold the door open for coworkers. Each instance of sharing yourself, even in small ways, is a blessing to brighten your day. The bonus is that almost imperceptibly, your giving becomes part of who you are. What a loving example that sets for others.

73

Accept that there are things you simply cannot change.

Time, the weather, computer viruses, income taxes—these are the topics that get a lot of press and stress. You can identify strategies to deal with their consequences, but you do not have absolute control over them. So avoid giving the gifts of your energy and time and emotions to issues that are beyond your control.

No. No. No. I will not give in to grumbling or feeling depressed about issues over which I have little or no control. Perhaps you want to develop that discipline as well. You are not responsible for solving every problem in the world, or in your community, or in your workplace. You are responsible for responding to your corner of the world. When you are committed to being the best that you can be in your vocation, you are contributing more to the world than when you are trying to scatter yourself over many problems. Contributing your energy, time, and gifts to what you believe is your calling yields a lasting peace.

Developing Your Personal Power and Influence With an Intelligent Heart

Dolly Madison, wife of our fourth U.S. president, was one of the most loved women in American history. Everywhere she went, she impressed. The old and the young, the rich and the poor, educated and uneducated—all seemed captivated by Mrs. Madison. At one point, she was asked about the power that she had over people. Her response? "Power over People? I have none. I merely love everyone."

Our personal power is often an unwrapped and an untapped gift. Maybe you think that influential people have power and influence because of money and good luck. Maybe they do. But there are a lot of people who have developed power and influence because of their personal skills and knowledge and because they love others and others love them. They sow that love by caring about and trusting others. As English clergyman and author John Henry Jowett once said, "Love is not a product to be manufactured; it is a fruit. It is not born of certain works; it springs out of certain relations. It does not come from doing something; it comes from being with Somebody."

One can be given some measure of power and influence as a result of position or authority, but this kind of power and influence doesn't last long if others perceive this person as lacking in credibility. A leader does not effectively lead by making others follow. A leader provides leadership because others willingly choose to follow. Leadership is more of lending a hand to pull one's constituency than shoving them in a particular direction. Effective leaders love and prove themselves trustworthy.

The following ideas provide strategies for developing your knowledge, skills, and personal trustworthiness so that others choose to respond to your guidance and influence. You can develop your leadership skills regardless of your current status, power, or position.

74

Discover your passion, and it will be your motivation for achieving your goals, no matter how lofty.

What is your passion in life? What is it about your goals that puts fire in your belly? What is it about your goals that makes you yearn to achieve them? What is it about reaching your goals that will give you a measure of peace?

Performer Ben Vereen had a life-threatening accident in 1992; he was expected to die. During a visit with Liza Minnelli he spoke of his shame about his condition. She reminded him that it was a miracle that he was alive. Then, impromptu, they began singing, "Accentuate the positive, eliminate the negative." That thought became Vereen's passion, which guided him to set high goals. Soon after, he was transferred to a rehabilitation center by wheelchair, and six months later he walked out. In 1993, Ben Vereen was back on a Broadway stage starring in *Jelly's Last Jam.**

75

Harness your passion for what you want to achieve by establishing goals in a rational manner.

So few people take the time to identify where they want to go and how they intend to get there that it is noticeable to others when you do. Establishing clear goals sends the message that you have a sense of direction and purpose.

Setting clear goals that are important to you also fuels your passion. According to C. Rick Snyder, a professor at the University of Kansas, establishing a goal can cause hopes of attaining it to soar. Sometimes just setting a goal can turn around a hopeless attitude. Bob Stone, coauthor of *Where the Buffaloes Roam,* was dying of cancer but decided he had a passion for living. Rather than allowing the word *cancer* to sound a death call, he mobilized his friends, family, and acquaintances who were showering him with love, concern, and pray-

*Robert McGarvey, "Pinning Goals on High Hopes," *KIWANIS* Magazine (February 1994).

ers into a team that would act as a life force. Day by day, week by week, calls, cards, banners, letters, and prayers poured in. Members of his team spanned the globe. Ten months later, his cancer was declared to be in remission. Bob is certain that the community of love that was built to strengthen him, strengthened them all and led to his wellness.†

76

Your life is a gift; you get to choose the direction that it will take.

What a beautiful and empowering thought. Establish your direction, and then write each of your goals to get there. Use specific, measurable, and focused terms so that you know when you have achieved each one. Writing each goal down changes it from a daydream to more of a commitment. Establishing your goals in a specific way jump-starts your achievement of them.

Stating to yourself, "I need to be in better shape" or "I want to do my best" is too general. Do you mean physically? Nutritionally? Emotionally? In your career? "I want to increase my upper body strength over the next three months" or "I want to get my next promotion in the next nine months" is much more specific, and you can measure the result.

---

†*Where the Buffaloes Roam: Building a Team for Life's Challenges,* © 1993 by Bob Stone and Jenny Stone Humphries. Published by Addison-Wesley Publishing Company, Inc.

77

Is your goal believable to you, even if others disagree with you?

If you can picture yourself achieving the steps to reach your goal, you probably will! Those of us who have high hopes and a strong will for achieving our goals shrug off the negativism of others. In fact, it's useful to avoid the naysayers and instead surround yourself with a network of support and encouragement.

A fellow consultant shares her perspective: "If I want to be 365 percent better at the end of the year than on January 1 of that year, that goal seems overwhelming. But if I consider being 1 percent better each day, that seems to be much more manageable." "I am free to be when I believe in me" seems to be a useful byline! Years ago on a television program, Muhammed Ali was heard saying, "If my mind can conceive it and my soul can believe it, then I can achieve it."

78

Set goals to stretch your talents and abilities.

Provide yourself with challenges to motivate yourself. If the goal is too easy or too hard, you'll come up with a dozen excuses for not getting started. And there often is as much joy in the progress toward the goal as the actual achievement.

Consider two or three of your goals. Write them down, and then do a challenge check. Are they challenging enough?

Worthy enough for the investment of your time and energy to achieve them?

_____

_____

_____

79

Establish a time frame for achieving your goal.

Often we don't move "off the dime" unless we mentally push ourselves with a time schedule. Decide how your time needs to be invested in order to progress toward the results that you want to achieve.

80

Keep your goals in harmony.

When goals are in conflict, our resources of time, energy, and money often are wasted and lead to feelings of failure and stress.

Beginning a business, having a second child, and continuing her education toward a doctorate began to take its toll on one woman. When questioned more closely about her goals and her feelings about them, she admitted that she had begun work on her doctorate years before, and she found that she was plodding along to accomplish it. But when she considered that goal and her goals of raising a family and making a success of her business, she decided that the pursuit of the doctorate was actually competing against other goals that had become more important to her. She quit school so that she could dedicate her time, energy, and talents to her higher-priority goals.

81

Stamp a large CANCEL on your negative self-talk.

Do you practice the art of losing? Many of us do, you know. We practice losing day in and day out by the way that we talk to ourselves.

Stop the incessant internal chatter that lowers your confidence, your hope, and your self-worth. You can choose to stop it. You can choose to replace the negativity with positivity. This is a personal discipline to cultivate, and you can do it.

Negative words to and about ourselves can be viewed as the weeds in our conversations. A friend who enjoyed casual gardening as one of her hobbies after long hours at work found that she had a hard time keeping up with the need to pull weeds. Well into spring, after having planted a garden of vegetables, the produce was growing, but the weeds were nearly out of control. One Saturday, she was on her hands and knees getting ready to deal with the weeds when a five-year-old neighbor walked over and surveyed her work. And he asked one question: "Did you know that you have to pull the weeds?" That's what we need to ask ourselves with regard to our self-talk. Have we pulled the weeds of negativism from our thoughts so that the positive self-talk can take root and flourish?

82

Seek to increase your responsibility, and ask for the accompanying increase in authority.

It's reasonable to expect authority that is commensurate with increased responsibility, but you may have to ask for it. Recently, a friend moved from her role as account supervisor to vice president of an advertising agency. She saw the opportunity to increase her responsibility and took it. Initially, the CEO and the president were reluctant to give her the parallel authority, but she insisted on it for the good of the company, and ultimately they agreed.

In what areas do you have responsibility but not the authority to get things done? How is this mismatch blocking the achievement of goals for your company or in your work? Once you respond to these questions, consider actions that you are willing to take to resolve this conflict.

_____

_____

_____

_____

83

Be right most of the time by using effective problem solving, decision making, priority setting, and planning skills.

Presenting data, facts, and logical argument builds your personal power and raises the probability that you will be heard.

When a needs analysis was being done at a power plant, managers were asked in interviews, "What employee do you most admire, and why?" When the name of one supervisor came up, the manager indicated that although she was not high on the organizational chart at this point, he fully expected her to do well because of her attention to setting effective goals and identifying problem areas and strategies for resolving them. "People just listen to this woman," he said, "because she comes well prepared and seems to know what she is talking about."

84

Consider your use of power when persuading others.

Few of us enjoy receiving orders; we'd rather have the latitude to figure out things for ourselves. So establish the guidelines of what is expected, the time frame, and the resources available, but encourage people to figure out their own methods for getting the results. When you frequently encourage others' input and avoid giving commands, people respond more favorably when you must use directives.

If someone were to ask you to raise your hand and place it palm-to-palm with theirs and then began to push, what would you do? Put your hand down? Allow yourself to be pushed? Or would you push back? Most people push back. They are not willing to be pushed around physically. And experience shows that most of us don't want to be pushed around emotionally either. We may appreciate guidance, but we want to figure out our own path to accomplish the goal.

85

Make friends and allies for your ideas and beliefs.

It's a smart thing to do if done in a fair and honest way. Building contingencies of support for your ideas makes good sense, and a bonus is that you build goodwill and respect.

Now we're talking about politics. Office politics. How do these two words make you feel? Although the term is neutral, we have feelings about it because of the way that people choose to use politics to reach their goals. When you choose to use politics in an honest, respectful way, office politics is a useful and positive strategy for building your personal power and influence.

86

Choose talented subordinates.

At home, in the community, and at work, surrounding your-self with strong and competent people reflects well on your decision making. Some people fear talented employees, worry-ing that subordinates may want the boss's job. Well, it's true. They do. But wouldn't most of us like a promotion that might mean getting our boss's job? Instead of fearing talent, capital-ize on it. Use others' talent as a means to achieving the kinds of results that will lead to advancing your career goals as well as organizational goals.

Mary Kramer, an Iowa state senator, reminds us that "the ability to develop and capitalize on the strengths of talented employees creates a pool of employees to which you can con-fidently delegate." She stresses the need to develop diverse tal-ent, not just clones of your own strengths and interests. If you are an idea person and a planner, you need to hire people who can carry out your ideas.

87

Increase your knowledge and skills.

You influence others by demonstrating a continuing willing-ness to learn and be taught. Develop a philosophy of "always becoming." In doing so, you build your reservoir of knowl-edge and experience, which contributes to higher-quality per-formance.

A colleague was commenting on someone we know in the training and development field: "He is a great guy, but he seems caught in a time warp. He hasn't kept pace with what is going on in management today. I just don't think that he has the credibility that he had twenty years ago." The journey of learning and growing helps us avoid the trap of obsolete skills.

88

Develop trustworthiness by identifying a win-win situation as much as possible.

Most of us dislike losing, yet we often create win-lose postures. A win-win perspective establishes that you are trying to care about the other person's needs as much as your own. So develop a reputation for fair and honest relationships. The more trustworthy that you are perceived to be, the less defensiveness you will see in others.

A study of forty-one executives, some of whom had made it to the top and some whose careers had been derailed, showed that all of them were very much alike except for one quality. Of those who had erred, the same mistake had led to that person's downfall: betraying a trust.

89

Demonstrate belief in your position through your conviction and enthusiasm.

Sometimes the facts and data are not enough. Others want to feel your passion for your position. Sincere enthusiasm is easily recognizable, and it quickly mobilizes attention. All other things being equal, the person who lives and breathes with enthusiasm is superior to the one who shows no passion.

Pauline is a creator and sculptor of Santas. Her many designs, all of them beautiful, are named, numbered, and carefully displayed. When she talks about her creations, she speaks of them lovingly, as though they are her friends. Those to whom she sells her Santas want them in part because they seek to share the goodwill and enthusiasm that Pauline exudes about her product. She sells her Santas through word of mouth, and in her third year of selling them, she sold 450, a 300 percent gain over her first year! Next year, she expects to sell 800 Santas.

There's really no substitute for a passionate belief in your work!

90

Seek to understand others.

Develop empathy for the other point of view. You probably will not influence others to any great degree unless they believe that you understand their needs and concerns. When you effectively respond, others will be more interested in listening to what you have to say.

Deciding to approach others with a perspective of how you can be helpful is an invitation for others to talk as you listen.

A marketing representative shared the anecdote of meeting with a group of salespeople who expressed anger, frustration, hurt, embarrassment, and humiliation over changes in their compensation and performance appraisal plans. Initially the meeting with them seemed to be going nowhere, but when the marketing representative expressed a willingness to hear and respond to their concerns instead of forcing her agenda, the group settled down, spoke rationally, and prioritized the issues of their position. As a result, there were positive outcomes to the meeting, salespeople expressed a recognition of the marketing rep's desire to understand them, and they expressed a new-found desire to be more helpful to her.

91

Choose your enemies carefully.

Are your enemies people? Or are they issues and challenges with which to deal? Are you fighting egos or injustices? Direct your anger toward causes that deserve it. Fight pain, cruelty, abusiveness, and deceit. Avoid tearing down individuals simply because they differ from you. Perhaps a helpful barometer is to ask yourself, "How is my anger benefiting the mission of this organization? How am I being helpful to the broader goal? Is my anger justified in the light of my belief system and values?"

Consider what makes you angry. After writing down two or three ideas, think about the degree to which your pride is involved versus a passion to right an issue that is wrong.

_____

_____

_____

92

Practice good timing.

You may be following most of these guidelines for influencing others, but if your timing is off, you may find yourself losing ground. Identify the most effective timing for making a request, giving a directive, or communicating a decision.

The company that gave a larger bonus than ever to its corporate heads in the same year that the union constituency was asked to drop their wage by a dollar an hour was not practicing good timing.

The new vice president of human resources who immediately started to make dramatic changes without first communicating with employees was not practicing good timing.

The university president who, without explanation, created two new vice-presidential positions in the same month that lower-level positions were eliminated was not practicing good timing.

Each of these decisions may have been useful, even vital, to organizational goals, but the need to consider the timing to take action was crucial.

$$\boxed{93}$$

Take others off the defensive by anticipating and meeting objections.

Find ways to avoid having others feel put down. A manager has discovered a way to control the rumor mill at her plant. Instead of simply telling culprits to stop spreading rumors, she instituted a rumor log. She keeps an account of the rumors and then identifies all those that don't come to pass. Instead of putting an employee on the defensive by arguing the accuracy of the information, she confronts the situation by keeping a log and then letting time prove the truth.

$$\boxed{94}$$

Use skillful assertive communication to increase your personal power and influence.

Assertive communication is honest and direct, and it also gives and expects respect. This includes being accepting and respectful of another's right to disagree with your point of view or what you do.

Several years ago, Anna received some helpful advice about accepting criticism in a more assertive way while involved in a train-the-trainer session. One of the requirements of the course was to present the course material to the rest of the participants. Since the information was new, Anna's presentation of the material wasn't as polished as it could be.

Later, in debriefing the session, the instructor offered her a suggestion for more assertive behavior: "If you ask for criticism, you'll get it. People want to give their opinions. Listen to them respectfully, but respect your own performance by using the 80–20 rule: Accept the useful 20 percent; let go of the rest of the criticism."

95

Cultivate the use of fair language.

How often do you hear broad generalizations? When communicating, avoid them. Narrow the scope of your assertions to make your communication more effective. Using phrases such as, "In my judgment" or "it has been my experience that" or "I understand that . . . ," are ways of owning your statements as your opinion, which reminds others that you know that there are more opinions than your own.

During a conversation about starting meetings on time among team members, one of the members asserted, "Well, I'm never late." Immediately a response came: "Never late? I remember one time when you were ten minutes late four months ago." The use of generalizations leads to nitpicking, digressions, and escalating issues that have little to nothing to do with the topic at hand. Avoiding their use is an effective communication strategy.

96

Admit your mistakes.

We seem to be conditioned against being vulnerable and admitting our mistakes, but it is empowering when you demonstrate the ability to recognize your mistakes. Consistently honest and respectful communication, with both the positive and the negative, establishes trust, which raises the probability that others will allow you to influence them. Admitting your wrongs and making apologies are cherished gifts to others.

During a meeting with staff to improve team relationships, the marketing director of a communications firm made this comment: "I know that I'm not the most communicative person. In fact, I don't compliment you or even converse with you as often as I should. I apologize. And I really want to change my ways." Her admission had a tremendous impact on her staff. They became more receptive to her efforts and more willing to make changes for the good of the department.

For the most part, people are not comfortable with those who wear a perfect persona because we intuitively know that no one is perfect. We tend to be drawn to those who openly admit their mistakes and have the courage to resolve them.

97

Share information.

In fact, share as much information as possible with others. Some people withhold information in order to feel more powerful, but, in reality, others perceive this behavior as weak and insecure. Sharing relevant information is powerful and viewed as a step in building trust.

The president of a realty firm found herself in conflict with a vice president. The two of them were willing to discuss their concerns with one another. The vice president sat silently while the president made sincere attempts to share information about the issues. Slowly a bridge of trust began to take form as each of them recognized the other's efforts to share information in an honest and forthright manner.

98

When supporting a position, make a point of identifying how your position benefits the organization and its goals in order to influence others.

Too often, the focus is on "what's in it for me." Sometimes by identifying what is best for the organization or the situation at hand, you give up allegiance to your ego and instead seek the good for the whole. The echo of your intentions will come back to you again and again.

An idea for putting this idea to work at the beginning of each day is to write the question, "What is the best use of my time and energy for meeting organizational goals?" at the top of a piece of paper and then list the actions to be taken.

99

Seek others' input when possible.

Others are better able to accept a position or a decision when they feel part of it. Your ability to be sensitive to others' needs raises the probability that others will be willing to work with you.

When a training program for self-directed work teams was implemented in a rehabilitation agency, initially both the union and management seemed to support it. About a year into the effort, though, the union representative began making negative comments about the success of teams. When she was confronted, she indicated that she as a union representative had felt left out of the loop in terms of planning and implementing the team training program. Once her input was sought, she began responding more positively to the team initiative and to the management of the facility.

100

If you ask for input, explain how you will use it in order to avoid misunderstandings.

If you are seeking information to consider but you intend to make the decision, solve the problem, or develop the plan, then say so. Otherwise people expect to have their input used.

A power plant that was instituting a new compensation plan scheduled required meetings for all employees to offer their opinions about the new plan. But employees were not told that a decision to implement the plan already had been made; hearing their opinions was just a vehicle for understanding how employees were thinking. The result was that employees felt cheated. They had attended the meetings with the understanding that their input would be used in the final decision. Several more meetings were required to clear up the conflict that would not have escalated had senior management been clearer about the purpose of the meetings.

101

Trust your instincts.

Often the information that seems to be from our "gut" is actually based on accumulated information from our experience. Even if it goes against the grain of a group, sometimes you have to act in accordance with what your gut tells you to do.

What are some of the pieces of wisdom that you have accumulated over the years that guide your speech and your actions?

_____

_____

_____

You'll discover that there are times when your instincts need to be the guiding light rather than strict adherence to the apparent facts.

102

In order to lead others through your influence, you must also serve.

A willingness to listen and respond to others' concerns is essential to others' willingness to follow you. Your service to others not only improves your leadership position, but it is viewed as kindness. In taking an initiative of service, our leadership becomes more apparent.

> "Wherever there is a human being there is an opportunity for kindness."
>
> —Seneca

103

If you present a problem, take the time to identify at least one solution, and more if possible.

People have enough problems; it is the solutions that they need and want to hear. When you can offer reasonable solutions to a problem, your concern probably will get the attention that you believe that it deserves. Furthermore, in the words of the lead character in *Forrest Gump,* "When you feel there is an unfair burden on your shoulders, that's just the way it is sometimes."

Trials at work can make you bitter or better; which do

you choose? Decision makers get tired of hearing a high proportion of problems. In fact, they start to hear the repetition of problems from so many employees as whining. Raise your value to your company by deciding to use problems to make your skills better. Problem solving, decision making, and planning all can be improved through facing a "good" problem!

104

Know yourself.

Know your strengths and your weaknesses. Capitalize on your strengths, and make a plan to improve your weaknesses. A great start to accepting others is to accept yourself first.

105

Give of yourself in ways that are meaningful to others.

If you give coveted basketball tickets to friends who hate basketball, the giving isn't especially meaningful. If you don't know what to give, ask. Both the giver and the receiver are happier with the act of giving when the gesture is truly meaningful.

Ask your employees this question: What can I do to show my appreciation for you in ways that are meaningful to you? Ask for ideas that cost nothing and ideas that might cost several dollars. Then suggest that employees ask this question of each other. The responsibility for appreciating each other is part of every employee's role. Sharing this responsibility balances power among people and encourages employees to develop the art of kindness.

106

Ground your decisions, statements, and ideas in a determination of moral action that aligns itself with your belief system of right and wrong.

An action may be legal, but perhaps in this day and age of law loopholes and legal gymnastics that is not the issue. An attorney expressed it this way: "If you have to ask the question, 'Is this ethical?' then you probably have your answer."

107

Honesty is the best policy.

Choose the action that would make you proudest to look at yourself in the mirror. Is yours a reflection that makes you feel proud?

Go ahead. Get a mirror or imagine looking into a pool of water. What do you see? What personal qualities are you proud of?

_____

_____

_____

What personal qualities would you like to develop?

_____

_____

_____

Your Intelligent Heart and Daily Work

MEETINGS

If each of five employees making a salary of $42,000 spends a minimum of five unproductive hours each week in meetings, $26,250 is lost annually. What better use could you have for that money? No matter what life's work we have chosen, most of us are required to attend meetings. And most of us believe that meeting time is time that could be better spent. Meetings are necessary, but there are strategies for increasing the likelihood that meetings you attend will be more productive and efficient.

108

Designate a meeting leader.

This is a wise decision in most meetings. This person is responsible for planning the meeting, setting up its agenda, and ensuring that the meeting goes according to plan. Without a leader, groups tend to flounder and waste time.

In one large corporation, several employees who are on a multifunctional team complain of their team leader, who calls regularly scheduled meetings that seem to have only one purpose: to have each member give a progress report of information that seems to be meaningful only to that team leader. During the meetings, members aren't listening closely; they don't recognize a value to the meetings because what gets done could be accomplished in a memo. As a result, this company loses time and money.

109

Prepare for your part in the meeting.

Consider your role as a meeting participant. Are you really needed? Do you contribute knowledge, skill, stature, and/or credibility to the meeting? If you don't have something of value to contribute, don't attend.

Evaluate the cost of your attendance at the meeting, and evaluate the total cost of the meeting. If the savings and/or earnings that accrue as a result of the meeting don't outweigh its cost, then perhaps the meeting needs to be cancelled.

"Dost thou love life? Then do not squander time, for that's the stuff life is made of."

—Benjamin Franklin

110

Use an agenda.

Meetings without agendas are likely to digress, ramble, waste time, and engender conflict. Establish an agenda that provides information about the participants (who), kind of meeting (what), location (where), time and date (when), items for discussion (how), and meeting purpose (why). If possible, send the agenda ahead of time to all participants.

A plant manager of an aluminum rolling mill stated that after a series of meeting effectiveness training sessions, productivity at meetings rose at least 50 percent as a result of three things: starting and ending on time, using an agenda, and having each person coming prepared for his or her part in the meeting.

111

Know your reasons(s) for meeting.

Typically people meet to share information, to plan, to evaluate data, to solve a problem, to make a decision, or to motivate in some way—each a legitimate reason for meeting. Make the purpose of your meeting clear so that participants are mentally prepared and so that they remain focused and on track.

"Meeting to build morale—that's ridiculous," scoffed one meeting participant. But it's not ridiculous if you need people's active and focused participation. If your group is argumentative, fractious, or concerned about a team conflict, you do need to pay attention. A group's inability to work effectively together can have grave consequences on the planning that they do or the decisions that they make. Money is wisely spent in designing a plan to assist groups in working together more effectively for the good of organizational goals.

112

Designate a person to take notes or minutes, and use a specific format.

Avoid assigning the leader this duty. Instead, make it a rotating responsibility so that no one person feels burdened and everyone contributes to the effectiveness of the meeting.

Taking meeting minutes is traditionally viewed as a burdensome task, but it can be made more pleasant by adopting a standard form that is easy to use. Minutes will be easier to record, and they will be more consistent.

113

Avoid interruptions.

Close doors, hold the telephone calls, and apply attention to the meeting so that interruptions are minimized. Interruptions take valuable time and often stop the flow of a meeting.

Avoiding interruptions sends a message of respect to meeting participants and makes more efficient use of time. "You are the most important people to me at this time" and "The purpose of this meeting is important" are two messages that are sent when you refuse to allow an interruption. Your consistent effort to respect others nurtures the seed of personal responsibility in those people for their work performance as well as their ability to get along with others.

114

Start on time.

When a meeting time is established and not followed, late-comers learn that they can get away with being late; and those who arrive on time often feel that their time is being wasted. Perhaps even worse, a message is sent that it is okay to be late, and more and more participants may act on that message. None of these beliefs is a productive start to a meeting.

"You are late" is a phrase many of us have heard at some point. Perhaps we mumble an apology or an excuse and sit down, sometimes too embarrassed to contribute to the meeting. The frequency of lateness and the ensuing tension seem to diminish when groups agree on methods for managing lateness regardless of who the person is. Some groups lock the door at the appointed starting time. Others throw soft balls as the latecomer enters the room. Others decide to fine the latecomer. Whatever their choice, the strategy, when used consistently, offers a moment of humor, and then the meeting continues.

115

End on time.

When you establish an ending time to a meeting and miss it, you run the risk of losing your audience. They may feel angry as you "steal" extra time from them or may mentally check out, making the extra time useless.

No matter how interesting the meeting or how electrifying the speaker, you have an implied contract with people that the meeting starts and ends at specific times. If you don't honor that contract, you lose credibility with meeting participants, *and* you run the risk of having them break their implied contract of attendance. If you believe that you need extra time, stop the meeting and take a moment to get the permission of the group to continue for a designated period. Most of the time, meeting participants will respond to your need when you show respect for the use of their time.

116

These two ideas for saving minutes, money, and morale are so important, they are worth saying again: Start on time! End on time!

Doing so establishes your credibility as an effective meeting leader or participant, and your credibility has an impact on the effectiveness of your meeting.

Hired to run a series of training programs on effective meetings management for an aluminum smelter, the trainer sent memos saying that the session would begin at 8:15 A.M. and conclude by 4:30 P.M. And the morning of the first day, she began promptly at 8:15 A.M. Four men came in at 8:25 A.M. and explained their lateness: "Usually, with meetings around here, if the memo says 8:15, you can nearly guarantee it'll be ten minutes later starting." The next day, the meeting began at 8:15 A.M. as announced, and all participants arrived on time. Later one of the men said to the trainer, "News travels fast. We heard that you really do start on time."

117

Evaluate the meeting.

Provide five or ten minutes of evaluation following each meeting so that each participant understands what parts of the meeting went well and what needs improvement. Most important, participants need closure on what was accomplished.

> "I've got a great ambition to die of exhaustion rather than boredom."
>
> —Angus Grossart

Use meetings to work hard. And avoid boredom.

118

Use meeting guidelines so that participants understand and agree to what is expected of them.

Guidelines that establish the starting and ending times, breaks, and suggestions for holding attention and participation provide clear expectations. If a guideline is not followed, the group is reminded of its original commitment. Effective and successful meetings are the responsibility of all in attendance, not just the designated leader.

The strategy of using meeting guidelines is successful for many companies. Several years ago, a large aluminum-producing corporation implemented meeting guidelines to be used as part of its total quality improvement program. The guidelines were posted all over the facility; they were even laminated on sheets of paper 2-feet by 3-feet. And employees did seem to respect their use. One of the reasons was that the adherence to the efforts for total quality improvement was part of their annual performance evaluation. The company had the wisdom to implement consequences for performance toward goals that were most important.

119

Be encouraging of other participants.

Often good ideas go unspoken because a participant felt uncomfortable speaking up, and no one asked for his or her input. Asking, "Do you have something to add?" often yields little from a participant who is reserved. Instead, try one of these suggestions to get the gold from quiet members of a group. Prior to the meeting, ask that person to do some research or thinking on the topic and to bring written notes to the meeting. Ask whether he or she is comfortable speaking or has a preference for you to give the information. Or when asking for an opinion, ask an open-ended question. "In your judgment, what else do we need to consider?" or "What else can you add?" invite opinion and reduce the perception that there is a right or wrong answer. Find ways to praise people for their contributions. Following these suggestions will raise the confidence of quieter members so that they become more vocal over time.

120

Listen carefully.

Listen so well that you can rephrase what was said if asked to do so. Consider taking notes, a discipline that often helps participants listen more effectively.

One of the reasons that people listen poorly is that they are concentrating more on what they want to say next than what is being said at the moment. When this happens to you, take a moment to jot your thoughts so that you are confident you will remember them, and then turn your attention back to the speaker.

Frequently, after this suggestion is made, pens and sheets of paper appear. Most of us don't intend to be rude through poor listening, but it does happen. By improving our listening skills, we improve the communication process.

121

Think about the anatomy of a meeting.

Most meetings include planning for a successful meeting, an introduction to the meeting, discussion of agenda items, a summary of the meeting, and an evaluation of the meeting. Even with short meetings, consideration of these ideas maximizes meeting effectiveness.

Think in a little more detail about each meeting segment. In the planning stage, the agenda is established, room arrangements are made, materials are prepared, and speakers are scheduled. During the introduction of the meeting, introductions are made, the purpose of the meeting is stated, guidelines are reviewed, previous minutes are read and accepted, and the agenda is distributed. Following the agenda includes adhering to the schedule and identifying and assigning responsibilities associated with agenda items requiring action. A summary of the meeting states what was accomplished and establishes the agenda for the next meeting. All members should participate in evaluating the meeting, in writing or verbally. Evaluation, as part of each meeting, improves the effectiveness of future meetings. During this brief portion, participants are thanked for their attendance and for their contributions.

122

Before attending a meeting, plan for the results that you want from it.

Within the parameters of good judgment and respect for others, pursue those results. If appropriate, schedule your issue(s) as part of the agenda. Recognize that the results you want often come in stages. You may not be able to get what you want in one meeting, but you can lay the groundwork for desired results.

COMMUNICATIONS

We engage in many communications daily, and improving them is an ongoing concern for most of us. However, much technology has impeded caring and effective communication. Fax machines, answering machines, computers, and voice mail increase efficiency but decrease personal touch. And that personal touch is part of what keeps us human and grounded as we face the challenges of our busy lives.

Courses in assertion, conflict resolution, handling difficult people, and interpersonal skills fill up quickly as people seek to improve their interactions with others. These courses are a testimonial to the concern we all have for building these skills. This section is not a full course on the subject, but it offers many useful and applicable suggestions related to effective interactions. These strategies will improve your ability to communicate openly, directly, and with caring.

123

Take personal responsibility for your communications.

It doesn't matter what your intent is when you are trying to communicate; what matters is the way that your communication is received. In a misunderstanding, avoid assuming that the other person is to blame. Ask yourself, "What did I say that may have led to this misunderstanding?"

Personal empowerment is a trendy topic. We are determined to "get" empowered, but are we willing to accept the fullness of empowerment? Employees want greater power. Does each of them realize that greater responsibility for using that power wisely is part of the empowerment package?

124

Use "I" messages.

When you feel, think, or have an opinion about something, own it by using "I" messages. Owning your statements builds your credibility and trustworthiness, reduces the potential for defensiveness, and improves the standard of communication. Go a step further: Before you send a message, be sure that it is specific. "I am annoyed that you have arrived fifteen minutes late this morning" is a more direct communication about what you are thinking than this statement: "Everyone knows that you are always late." This first example gives clear and specific information. The second statement is general and vague, uses absolutes, and is nearly guaranteed to start an argument!

125

When you have something to say, say it.

Use statements when you want your opinions understood. Frequently people soften what they want to say by asking a question. "Do you want to go out for Chinese food?" invites a response of either yes or no. If your goal is to go out for Chinese food, then state it, and you raise the probability of agreement.

"Can you help me with this report?" one employee asked another. "No, I can't," was the response. And the person who asked the question was offended. There is an implied invitation to say yes or no when a question is asked in that way. If you ask a binary question, you may get an answer that you don't want. You reduce the probability that this will happen by using statements to express yourself.

126

Regularly make eye contact when you are speaking or listening.

A skilled speaker stood up to make a presentation to an audience of about twenty. She spoke confidently and knowledgeably for five minutes and then began to falter. By the time she finished, she seemed to retreat from the group. When asked, "What happened? You had such a great start." she gave a surprising reply. "I felt good about my preparation and what I was saying, but when I looked up different times, I noticed one person not giving me eye contact. He was looking around, or reading notes, or fiddling with his nails. I just couldn't make eye contact; his behavior told me that he was bored. My confidence just withered."

127

Be aware of what your body language is conveying.

A recent library slip indicated an overdue charge. Further scrutiny suggested a mistake on the part of the library. Walking up to the librarian, I said, "Hi, I'd like to argue this overdue charge." Quickly realizing my defensive language, I stopped to apologize and restated, "I mean, I'd like to discuss this overdue charge." The librarian chuckled. "I didn't even notice that you used the word *argue*. What I noticed was your smile and that you seem relaxed. Yours just sounded like a polite question to me."

> "We all, in one way or another, send our little messages out to the world. . . . And rarely do we send our messages consciously. We act out our state of being with nonverbal body language."
>
> —Julius Fast

128

Strengthen your speech by avoiding the use of "uhms" and "ahs."

Excessive use of these sounds bores an audience and dilutes the strength of your message.

In meetings of an international speaking organization,

one member is designated the "ah counter." This person keeps track of the number of times that "ahs," "uhms," or "uhs" occur. And what a useful exercise! Having a greater awareness of speech habits helps to cure the poor ones and enhance the strong ones.

129

Think about what you want to say before you open your mouth.

Have you ever suffered from a foot in the mouth? Sometimes it seems that we take that skill to an art form! But you can avoid embarassing verbal blunders by thinking before speaking. As well, think through what you want to say so that you maintain your credibility and the interest of your audience. Frequently, a speaker makes a statement and then for the next few minutes spends the time saying, "What I really mean is . . ."

A useful self-discipline is to ask yourself, "What exactly do I want to say?" Plan your communication with one other person just as you would in a letter, a meeting of several, or a presentation for several hundred. Many times people bemoan the misunderstandings that occur between people. But there's quite a difference in the breadth of meaning when someone says, "I guess that plan will work," versus the person who states, "Most of the plan seems intact, but please strengthen the language in stating your purpose and establish cost figures for each step of the plan." The second statement helps the listener zero in on what needs to be changed.

130

Gauge the temperature of your language.

Audiences, whether of one or of one hundred, tend to be offended by vulgarity, sexism, and/or racial remarks. The language that we choose to use in the presence of others sends a message about our respect for ourselves and for them. Besides being unattractive, the use of inconsiderate language communicates a limited vocabulary and limited thinking.

An executive in a communications firm had a reputation for his fiery vulgarities and coarse outbursts—a habit that stood in stark contrast to his many assets. His intelligence, his good looks, his energy, and his sense of humor were well-developed qualities, but his language seemed to overshadow his other skills. When this contrast was pointed out to him, he made a decision to make a change. Four months later, he was able to say that he had gone four months without an outburst and had diminished his use of foul language dramatically. What a difference the change made in others' perceptions of him. Raising his standard of speech has meant an increase in his personal influence.

131

View yourself from a position of personal strength.

Avoid self-putdowns such as, "I'm not sure I can handle this," or "I don't have much experience with this." Instead, focus on the positive. Statements such as, "I enjoy a challenge," or "I'll come to you if I have any questions," provide a more positive perspective. And your consistently positive perspective strengthens others' perception of your confidence and abilities.

> "What you can't get out of, get into wholeheartedly."
>
> —Mignon McLaughlin

132

Consider sharing information about yourself.

When others are sharing background information, decide what information you are willing to share. People generally enjoy knowing some personal information about those with whom they interact. Information that tells others something about you is appropriate and helps to establish a rapport.

> "It's entirely in your power to regulate the degree to which you peel back the layers of your personality when you disclose yourself to someone. You can keep that person on the surface, or you can allow her to penetrate, by degrees or directly, to the core."
>
> —Harriet Braiker

we avoid the joy of giving and receiving in love? Do we wrap the protective coverings around our hearts so tightly that we lose touch with the feelings and vulnerability that help us to connect with one another?

It's certainly of economic importance to be competent, but there is an even higher value in the spiritual impact of behaving with compassion and in love. And that compassion, that reaching out to others in the strength of love, results from the intelligent heart. I wrote this book because I know the value of trying to live these ideas. I've learned and applied them bit by bit. The joy of moments when the waves of working compassionately as well as competently merge wells up beyond explanation, and it is with renewed energy that I pursue that wave again and again. Over the years, the fruits from the union of compassion and intellect have been greater joy, peace, patience, contentment, and self-control. And there is more to learn, and more to give, and more to gain. The intelligent heart lives from a spirit of abundance, not scarcity.

Bibliography

Alberti, Robert E., and Michael L. Emmons. *Your Perfect Right—A Guide to Assertive Living.* San Luis Obispo, Calif.: Impact Publishers, 1990.

Autry, James A. *Love and Profit—The Art of Caring Leadership.* New York: Avon, 1991.

Bolton, Robert. *People Skills.* Englewood Cliffs, N.J.: Prentice Hall, 1979.

Covey, Steven R. *The 7 Habits of Highly Effective People—Powerful Lessons in Personal Change.* New York: Fireside, 1989.

Exley, Helen, ed. *The Best of Business Quotations.* Mount Kisco, N.Y.: Exley Publications, 1993.

Fast, Julius. *Body Language.* New York: Pocket Books, 1971.

Groom, Winston. *The Wit and Wisdom of Forrest Gump.* New York: Pocket Books, 1994.

Kouzes, James M., and Barry Z. Posner. *The Leadership Challenge.* San Francisco: Jossey-Bass, 1987.

McGarvey, Robert. "Pinning Goals on High Hopes." *Kiwanis Magazine* (February 1994).

McGinnis, Alan Loy. *Bringing Out the Best in People—How to Enjoy Helping Others Excel.* Minneapolis: Ougsburg Publishing House, 1985.

Stein, Melissa, ed. *The Wit and Wisdom of Women.* Philadelphia: Running Press, 1993.

Stone, Bob., and Jenny Stone Humphries. *Where the Buffaloes Roam: Building a Team for Life's Challenges.* Reading, Mass.: Addison-Wesley, 1993.

Waitley, Dr. Denis. *The Psychology of Winning—Ten Qualities of a Total Winner.* New York: The Berkley Publishing Group, 1979.

Wallace, Amy, David Wallechinsky, and Irving Wallace. *The People's Almanac Presents The Book of Lists #3.* New York: Morrow, 1983.

Weems Jr., Lovett H. *Church Leadership: Vision, Team, Culture, and Integrity.* Nashville, Tenn.: Abingdon Press, 1993.

A personal note to the women who wish to live and love life more fully . . .

What experiences have helped *you* develop your intelligent heart?

If you have other nuggets of wisdom about your personal journey to develop your intelligent heart, please send them. Women often have shared their insights and stories with me. I'd like to hear from you as well.

Please write to me in care of: AMACOM Books, 135 West 50th Street, New York, NY 10020. The sharing of experiences adds richness to our journey. I look forward to hearing from you.

Susan B. Wilson

Your Pages:
Notes About Your Journey
to an Intelligent Heart

Notes

Notes

Notes

Notes

Notes

Notes

Notes

Notes